4 Ingredients

kids

Also by Kim McCosker

4 Ingredients ONE POT, ONE BOWL
Rediscover the Wonders of Simple, Home-Cooked Meals

4 Ingredients CHRISTMAS
Recipes for a Simply Yummy Holiday

BABY BOWL
Home-Cooked Meals for Happy, Healthy Babies and Toddlers

By Kim McCosker and Rachael Bermingham

4 Ingredients
More than 400 Quick, Easy, and Delicious Recipes
Using 4 or Fewer Ingredients

4 Ingredients GLUTEN-FREE
More than 400 New and Exciting Gluten-Fr
Using 4 or Fewer Ingredients

4
Ingredients
kids
Simple, Healthy Fun in the Kitchen

Kim
McCosker

ATRIA PAPERBACK

New York   London   Toronto   Sydney   New Delhi

ATRIA PAPERBACK

A Division of Simon & Schuster, Inc.
1230 Avenue of the Americas
New York, NY 10020

First Atria Paperback edition August 2013

ATRIA PAPERBACK and colophon are trademarks of Simon & Schuster, Inc.

For more information about food safety, visit www.foodsafety.gov.

For information about special discounts for bulk purchases,
please contact Simon & Schuster Special Sales at
1-866-506-1949 or business@simonandschuster.com.

The Simon & Schuster Speakers Bureau can bring authors
to your live event. For more information or to book an event,
contact the Simon & Schuster Speakers Bureau at
1-866-248-3049 or visit our website at www.simonspeakers.com.

Photography by Stuart Quinn Photography

Manufactured in China

10 9 8 7 6 5 4 3 2 1

Library of Congress Cataloging-in-Publication Data
McCosker, Kim.
  4 ingredients kids : simple, healthy fun in the kitchen / Kim McCosker.
     pages   cm
Includes index.
1. Quick and easy cooking. 2. Children—Nutrition.
I. Title. II. Title: Four ingredients kids.
TX833.5M429   2013
641.5'55—dc23   2012048263

ISBN 978-1-4516-7799-7
ISBN 978-1-4516-7800-0 (ebook)

Contents

Contents

PARTY TIME!

Introduction

Hello, moms and dads! Welcome to *4 Ingredients Kids*! As we all know, a child's appreciation of delicious, healthy food begins at home. If you like to eat great meals, they will too! If you enjoy cooking, they'll want to get their grubby little hands in the kitchen as well. And the more they get involved in food preparation, the more likely it will be that they at least *try* whatever scrumptious bites are brought to the table. If any of you are familiar with my previous books, *4 Ingredients*, *4 Ingredients Gluten-Free*, *4 Ingredients Christmas*, or *4 Ingredients One Pot, One Bowl*, you know that I'm all about clever cooking and entertaining. Who wants to spend all day preparing and cleaning up after a meal when you could be eating, playing, and enjoying life with everyone you love?

4 Ingredients Kids features eighty quick, easy, and delicious recipes that require only four ingredients and are designed to excite kids (of all ages!) and to encourage participation in the kitchen. (Special note: Salt, pepper, and water are not included in the four ingredients.) In these lovely pages, you'll also find sections on healthy eating habits, kitchen safety and hygiene, and loads of party ideas, all tested and approved by my three little boys, Morgan, Hamilton, and Flynn.

To put this book together, my invaluable 4 Ingredients team and I turned to social media and asked you, our wonderful readers, which recipes kids in the big wide world love, which ones parents currently have in their repertoires, most-requested meals, and which dishes your kids have made themselves. The most popular recipes, the ones mentioned over and over again, are what comprise this cookbook. Think Spaghetti Cupcakes, Partysicles, Dinosaur Eggs, Pizzadillas, and Taco Popcorn. Think smiles, fun, and full tummies for even the fussiest eaters. Think fewer ingredients, fewer utensils, less cleanup, and more time spent with family.

Kids are 30 percent of our population but 100 percent of our future. It's up to us to arm them with the skills to nourish their bodies. Teaching our kids how to eat well and how to cook shouldn't be a chore—it's a gift. My hope is that *4 Ingredients Kids* becomes a happy, go-to guide for your home and loved ones.

With love,
Kim

Cooking Made Easy: A Brief Glossary of Terms

Be prepared for questions if your little ones are "assisting" you in the kitchen. Stage your own cooking show and make use of this cheat sheet to describe the steps in each recipe.

Al dente: Often found in pasta recipes. It means to cook the pasta just until it's done, not soft or overcooked.

Au gratin: Refers to a baked dish, such as a casserole, topped with cheese or bread crumbs, then browned on top, either in the oven or under a broiler.

Baste: To spoon or brush food with a liquid—such as butter, broth, or the cooking liquid—to help the food stay moist during cooking.

Blanch: To place food briefly in boiling water and then plunge into cold water to halt cooking. Blanching is also used to loosen the skins of fruits and vegetables to help peel them more easily.

Boil: The boiling process serves two purposes. It destroys organic impurities, and it transforms raw ingredients into cooked foods. Interestingly, boiling water is affected by altitude. The higher you climb, the lower the boiling point. Water boils at sea level at 212°F.

Braise: To slowly cook browned foods in a small amount of liquid in a tightly covered pot.

Brown: To brown meat means to cook until browned on the surface. You may brown the outsides of a roast on the stovetop before cooking in a slow cooker or oven.

Butterfly: Splitting meat, poultry, or fish in half horizontally without cutting all the way through. When spread open, the flat piece looks like a butterfly.

Caramelize: Melting and cooking sugar over low heat until it browns. Caramelization also refers to the browning that occurs during cooking.

Chiffonade: Thinly sliced strips or shreds of vegetables or herbs.

Cream: To rapidly mix one or more ingredients with a spoon or mixer until smooth and creamy. When you cream butter or other fats, the mixture also becomes fluffy because air is incorporated during the rapid mixing process.

Curdle: A mixture curdles when it separates into a liquid with solid particles. For example, soured milk curdles.

Deglaze: To add a liquid to a pan in which food has been browned and stir it over heat to loosen the cooked food particles. This liquid is usually thickened to make a flavorful sauce.

Dice: To dice is like to chop, but the pieces are smaller.

Dredge: To dredge is to coat a food lightly with flour, bread crumbs, or cornmeal.

French: To cut meat or vegetables lengthwise into very thin strips.

Grate: To reduce to fragments, shreds, or powder by rubbing against an abrasive surface, often a kitchen tool called a "grater."

Julienne: To cut a fruit or vegetable into match-stick strips about 2 inches long.

Marinate: To soak food in a mixture of spices, oil, and often an acid (like wine or vinegar) to make it more tender and flavorful. You can generally marinate food for 30 minutes and up to a day or two, depending on the dish.

Mince: To cut food into very fine pieces.

Reduce: To boil a liquid in an uncovered pot or pan to evaporate some of the liquid. This reduces the volume, con-centrates the flavor, and thickens the mixture.

Sauté: To cook a food, while stirring, in a small amount of fat over direct heat.

Score: To make shallow cuts in the surface of a food just before cooking or baking.

Sear: To quickly brown the surface of a food, using high heat, to seal in the juices. Foods can be seared in a very hot pan or under the broiler.

Slice: To cut completely through an object. Think of slicing cheese, bread, meat, and fruit.

Simmer: To slowly cook food in a liquid just below the boiling point. Tiny bubbles may break the surface.

Steam: To cook foods using moist heat, under varying degrees of pressure.

Steep: To soak dry ingredients in a hot liquid to infuse it with flavor and color, as with tea or coffee.

Sweat: To cook food over low heat in a small amount of fat in a covered pot or pan so it cooks in its own juices until soft but not browned.

Zest: The thin colored outer layer of citrus peels, which contains flavorful oils. Note: The white pith is not part of the zest and has a bitter taste.

Kitchen Safety & Hygiene Tips for Kids

Set the ground rules before your child picks up his first whisk or spatula!

Clean Hands

The first line of defense against germs is to WASH YOUR HANDS! Doing so prevents many illnesses, from the common cold to more serious conditions, such as meningitis, bronchiolitis, influenza, hepatitis A, and most types of infectious diarrhea.

Supervision

With knives, appliances, and heat sources in the kitchen, adult supervision is a must for any cooking activity with kids. An adult can help assess the potential dangers and ensure that children use kitchen equipment properly and practice all of the kitchen safety rules.

Restricted Activities

Kitchen activities should be age appropriate. Assess your child's age and maturity level to determine which kitchen duties should be restricted for them. Younger kids shouldn't handle sharp knives, but they might be able to handle a dull butter knife if it will do. If a sharp knife is necessary, an adult should handle the cutting. The use of the stove and oven should be reserved for older kids.

Proper Utensil Usage

Kids need to practice using all kitchen utensils and appliances properly. Demonstrate how to use spatulas, whisks, and egg beaters. Think about the types of utensils you use on a regular basis in the kitchen and include them in the demonstration. Do the same with small appliances, such as mixers, blenders, and toasters.

Food Handling

Kids also need guidance on proper food handling. If they are helping with meals that involve meat, instruct them on the importance of washing their hands and the work area after preparation. Emphasize that no other foods should go on the surfaces until they are clean. Storing cold foods in the refrigerator is another important lesson for the kids. Teach them to put leftovers in the refrigerator right away so harmful bacteria can't grow.

Cleaning

Cleaning the kitchen properly is a matter of safety that kids should address. Leaving remnants of food can lead to contamination of other food items. Show kids how to clean surfaces and remind them to clean immediately after finishing each task. Discuss where different waste materials go. If you have a compost bin, teach them which items go in it. If you recycle, talk to the kids about the packaging and items that can be reused or recycled.

Plastic Utensils

Plastic spatulas, measuring cups, bowls, and dishes are much easier for small hands to manage, so have plenty of those available.

Kitchen Best Practices

- Always turn pot or pan handles inward when cooking on the stovetop—away from prying fingers.
- Never place hot food or drinks on a surface that kids can reach.
- Always have an adult present for the "unexpecteds!"
- Keep it simple and have fun!

Healthy Habits for Healthy Kids

The United States Department of Agriculture (USDA) suggests basing a child's diet on the five food groups. To stay healthy, it's recommended that you and your children eat a certain number of servings from each of these groups every day.

FOOD GROUP	DAILY SERVINGS
Vegetables	5 servings
Grains (breads, cereals, rice, pasta, and noodles)	5–9 servings
Fruit	2 servings
Dairy (milk, yogurt, and cheese)	2–4 servings
Protein (Meat, fish, poultry, eggs, nuts, and legumes)	1–2 servings

Source: www.cnpp.usda.gov/Publications/MyPyramid/OriginalFoodGuidePyramids/FGP/FGPPamphlet.pdf.

It now seems appropriate to introduce you to a dear friend and colleague, Mr. Veggie Smuggler (Mr. VS). He will appear regularly throughout this book with ideas on how to incorporate (or smuggle!) more veggies into everyday meals in ways your kids won't even notice. ☺

❄ Also look for this icon, indicating which recipes can be frozen.

Food Safety

One in six Americans will get sick from food poisoning this year. Food poisoning is a serious public health threat in the United States. In fact, the Centers for Disease Control and Prevention (CDC) estimates that a whopping 48 million people get food poisoning each year, resulting in roughly 128,000 hospitalizations and 3,000 deaths.

Practice these 4 simple rules daily, and healthy habits will thrive in your family's home.

CLEAN: Wash your hands with warm soapy water for 20 seconds, or wash hands and surfaces often.

SEPARATE: Don't cross-contaminate. Clean cutting boards with hot soapy water after using for raw meat, poultry, or fish and before placing ready-to-eat food on it.

COOK: Color and texture are unreliable indicators of safety. Using a food thermometer is the only way to ensure the safety of meat, poultry, seafood, and egg products. These foods must be cooked to a safe minimum internal temperature to destroy any harmful bacteria.

CHILL: Do not leave food at room temperature for more than two hours (one hour when the temperature is above 90°F). Refrigerate leftovers promptly.

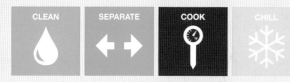

Look for these icons throughout this book and the simple Food Safety tip that accompanies them. *Prevention is the best cure.*

An Active Life

Childhood obesity is one of the most serious public health challenges of the twenty-first century. You've probably all heard the statistics from around the world; a quick Google search tells you that 1 in 4 children in Australia and the UK are overweight, 1 in 3 in the United States, and rates are growing at an alarming pace.

While many factors contribute to this, here are some practical suggestions we have learned to help fight obesity from a variety of both health experts and active families.

1. Play: Encourage your kids and grandkids to get at least 60 minutes of physical activity every single day. Cut down on sitting at the computer or in front of the television for more than 30 minutes at a time.

2. Let them have their say: Get your children involved in planning your weekly menus. The more input and interest they display, the greater the likelihood you have of getting them to eat their meals (or at least to try them).

3. Unplug: We know it's so very hard to turn off the TV and leave the iPhone or iPad in the office for meals, but please try to have at least one sit-down meal every day together as a family. Use this as your time for conversation and connection.

4. Keep healthy snacks handy: Keep a supply of nutritious snack foods like fruit, veggies, nuts, whole-grain crackers, breads, and cereals on hand. Cut them into bite-size pieces to make them more inviting. A child is more likely to grab a piece of watermelon than a whole watermelon!

5. Monkey see, monkey do: Set a good example by serving reasonable portions, eating lots of fresh fruits and vegetables, drinking lots of water, and exercising daily.

6. Eat breakfast: Of all the meals, do not skip brekky as it is the most important meal of the day. Not only is it linked to better brain function in kids, it also jump-starts their metabolism.

7. Focus on the quality, not the quantity: Never fear that your child isn't getting enough to eat. Trust your kid's appetite.

8. Don't give up: It may take several tries to get your kids to taste a new food. Keep it fun and relaxed!

You will find tags like the ones below throughout this book. You can use them to access enhanced digital content. To do so, simply download the free app at gettag.mobi. Then hold your phone's camera a few inches away from the tag and enjoy what comes next.

If you access content through a mobile device, message and data rates may apply.

Click to watch Kim chat with her kids about their favorite recipes.

(Page 14) Click and Bake these mouthwatering eggs with Kim and Hamilton.

(Page 54) Click and Cook these yummy Spaghetti Cupcakes with Kim.

(Page 62) Click and Cook this hearty stir-fry with Kim and Morgan.

(Page 68) Click and Cook this gooey mac 'n' cheese with Kim.

(Page 82) Click and Cook these tender lamb chops with Kim and Dylan.

(Page 84) Click and Cook these tasty chicken fingers with Kim.

(Page 112) Click and Make this decadent fudge with Kim.

(Page 122) Click and Bake these colorful cookies with Kim and Flynn.

(Page 128) Click and Bake these chewy M&M's bars with Kim and Ava.

(Page 146) Click and Make these gorgeous Chocolate Fruit Jewels with Kim and Ava.

(Page 170) Click and Cook these delicious sausages with Kim.

What's 4 Brekky?

A Breakfast Box

If I've heard it once, I've heard it a million times: "Breakfast is a very important meal. It's the fuel our bodies need to kick-start our busy days."

Serves 2

- *1 small banana, sliced*
- *8 strawberries, quartered*
- *¾ cup vanilla yogurt*
- *½ cup granola, plus extra for topping*

Layer the ingredients into a parfait dish or pretty box beginning with the fruit, then yogurt, and then cereal. Repeat two more times to finish with a layer of cereal on top. Top with a strawberry or berry of choice.

*Tip: Serve with a nutritious shake like our **Banana-Bix Shake:** 1 banana, 1½ cups milk, 1 Weetabix (or 2 to 3 tablespoons of your kids' favorite whole-grain cereal), and 1 teaspoon honey. Blend all the ingredients together until nice and smooth.*

Berry Blast

Serves 1

- ½ cup berry muesli
- ½ cup apple juice
- ½ green or Pink Lady apple, grated
- 2 tablespoons yogurt

In a small bowl, soak the muesli and apple juice overnight. In the morning, stir in the grated apple and yogurt.

Optional: Garnish with blueberries or any seasonal berry.

The nicest thing you can wear is a smile.

—Grandma

Brekky Bars

Makes 12

- *1½ cups quick-cooking oats*
- *¼ cup whole wheat flour*
- *¼ cup mango or apricot nectar*
- *1½ cups grated apple*

Preheat the oven to 350°F. Line a 3 by 7-inch bar pan with parchment paper. In a medium bowl, combine the oats, flour, nectar, and apple. Wet your hands and begin to mix. Mixing this way will help extract additional juice from the apples. Press the mixture into the pan, smoothing the top with the back of a spoon. Bake until golden, 25 to 30 minutes. Remove from the baking pan and cut into bars while still warm.

Optional: Add ½ cup raisins or chopped dates and sprinkle with your kid's favorite spice.

 CLEAN

Your hands normally carry lots of germs and should be washed regularly throughout the day, especially before or after handling food.

Cheesy Hash Browns

There is just something about the crispy deliciousness of homemade hash browns! My kids and I love them, and we often make double and freeze half to eat at a later date.

Makes 12 ❄

- *4 potatoes, peeled*
- *1 ¼ cups grated Cheddar cheese*
- *¼ cup vegetable oil, plus extra if needed*

Preheat the oven to 325°F. Line a baking sheet with paper towels. Coarsely grate the potatoes, then use your hands to squeeze out as much excess liquid as possible and transfer to a bowl. Stir in the Cheddar and season to taste. In a large nonstick skillet, heat 2 tablespoons of the oil over medium heat until shimmering but not smoking. Place four ¼-cup portions of the potato mixture in the pan and flatten each with a spatula. Cook until browned on one side, about 2 minutes. Flip and cook the other side for an additional 2 minutes. Transfer the hash browns to the baking sheet and place in the oven to keep warm. Repeat with the remaining mixture for 2 more batches, reheating and adding more oil between batches if necessary.

 Use this recipe to smuggle more delicious veggies into your kid's diet! Grate in a little onion, carrot, or zucchini, or add some finely chopped red or green bell pepper, or ham. All are healthy additions to the humble hash brown!

Green Eggs & Ham

I won't be quite as forceful as "Sam I Am," but I will encourage all kids, everywhere, to *just try* different foods. Without trying, how will they ever know the wonderful textures and flavors they're missing out on?

Serves 1

- *1 egg*
- *1 slice whole-grain bread*
- *1 thin slice honey-baked ham, cut into slivers*
- *1 teaspoon chopped fresh chives*

Heat an 8-inch nonstick skillet over low heat. In a small bowl, whisk the egg and 2 tablespoons of water until light and fluffy. Toast the bread while you cook the egg, as the egg cooks very quickly! Pour the egg into the skillet and stir constantly for about 1 minute, or until it becomes slightly firm. Stir in the ham and chives. Your egg is ready when there are no runny bits! Serve with the toast.

 If you have no chives, use parsley, the world's most popular herb, and a giant in terms of health benefits. Plant some herbs in small pots with your child; mint is a great herb to plant, as it is very hard to kill!

Purple Pancakes

One of the things I remember fondly about growing up was Saturday morning pancakes. My brothers and I cooked lots of pancakes, adding all sorts of yummy fillings; it was experimental and it was fun!

Makes 10

- *1 cup self-rising flour*
- *1 cup milk*
- *1 egg, beaten*
- *½ cup mixed berries*

In a bowl, lightly whisk together the flour, milk, and egg until all lumps are gone. Gently stir in the berries. Heat a nonstick skillet over medium heat. Using a ¼-cup measure, pour 3 lots of batter into the pan. Once the pancakes begin to bubble evenly, flip and cook the other side until the bottom is lightly golden. Repeat until all the batter is gone.

Optional: Serve dolloped with your kids' favorite yogurt and additional berries. If you have ground cinnamon in your pantry, add a pinch to the batter for a lovely flavor.

Volcanic Eggs

This is my boys' favorite style of "eggs on toast." Hamilton (my middle boy) was six when he drew the volcanic landscape on the inside of a copier-paper box . . . too cute!

Makes 4

- *4 eggs, separated*
- *4 slices whole wheat bread, crusts removed*
- *1 cup grated Parmesan cheese*

Preheat the oven to 350°F. In a bowl, with an electric beater, beat the egg whites until stiff peaks form. Using a sharp knife, cut large circles from each bread slice and place on a baking sheet. Spoon a mound of egg white onto each, then make a little crevice on the very top and gently place the egg yolk in it. Sprinkle with Parmesan and a grind of black pepper (the volcanic ash). Bake until the egg white is firm, the cheese melted, and the egg yolk runny when you cut into it (molten lava), 8 to 12 minutes.

 Click and Bake these mouthwatering eggs with Kim and Hamilton.

Artist: Hamilton Turnbull

Snack
Attack

Apricot Baskets

My "Poppy" used to have a stone fruit orchard. My earliest memories are of him picking an apricot, running his finger around its crease, flicking out the pit, and sharing, one half for him and one half for me. I would have been four or five at the time. Poppy is long gone, but this memory is as vivid in my mind as if it were yesterday.

Serves 4

- 4 fresh apricots, halved and pitted
- ¼ cup cottage cheese
- 1 teaspoon ground cinnamon
- 2 tablespoons honey

Fill each apricot half with cottage cheese. Add a sprinkle of cinnamon and drizzle with the honey.

Tip: Apricots are low in sodium, calories, and fat. They are high in vitamins A and C and are a good source of potassium. The fruit also contains phosphorus, iron, fiber, and calcium. Choose fresh apricots that are well formed, plump, and fairly firm. Refrigerate ripe apricots or if not ripe yet, ripen at room temperature in a brown paper bag with a banana or an apple.

Dinosaur Eggs

Once upon a time when I was making these in my kitchen, my beautiful then five-year-old came in, looked up quizzically at me, and said, "Mum, they look like dinosaur eggs!" No longer were they Apricot Balls, but forevermore Dinosaur Eggs!

Makes 40

- *2½ cups finely shredded coconut*
- *14 ounces dried apricots, finely chopped*
- *1 can (14 ounces) condensed milk*

Measure out ½ cup of the coconut and set aside on a wide, flat plate. Place the remaining coconut in a bowl and stir in the apricots and condensed milk. With wet hands, roll 2 teaspoons of the mixture into a "dinosaur egg" and roll in the reserved coconut. Refrigerate or freeze.

Edible Veggie Bowl & Dip

Serves 4

- *1 pound butternut squash, peeled and cut into 1½-inch cubes*
- *½ cup cashews*
- *3 tablespoons grated Parmesan cheese*
- *1 red bell pepper*

Preheat the oven to 350°F. Place the squash on a baking sheet and bake until golden in color and soft in texture, about 20 minutes. Allow to cool, then transfer the roasted squash to a food processor and add the cashew nuts and Parmesan and blend until combined. Season to taste with sea salt and pepper. Meanwhile, halve the bell pepper crosswise and remove the seeds and membrane. Keeping the bottom half as your "edible bowl," cut the other half into dipping sticks (notice I used some carrot and celery too—see photo). Spoon the dip into the bowls, and then add the dippers to decorate.

 Keep nutrition fun so kids will enjoy being healthy. Be creative! For example, a slice of carrot may be met with more enthusiasm when called a "carrot chip" or if used as eyelashes in an edible veggie bowl.

 SEPARATE *There are very few meals made without using a cutting board. If yours gets excessively worn or develops hard-to-clean grooves, consider replacing it, as those grooves often house unwanted bacteria.*

Play Date Buddies

These are a fun addition to any lunch box, or you can use the same idea for gorgeous party bags filled with candy, fresh or dried fruit, popcorn, cereal, or crackers!

Makes 2

- *3 ounces green grapes*
- *3 ounces red grapes*
- *¼ cup popped popcorn*
- *8 pretzels*

Into two resealable plastic snack bags place the grapes in one side and the popcorn and pretzels on the other. Clamp them in the center with a clothespin.

Tip: To make these, you will also need a few crafts bits 'n' bobs: wooden clothespins, colored pipe cleaners, paint, and stick-on googly eyes (or you can draw your own). I also use the clothespin "buddies" to hang my boys' artwork from a piece of string in their bedrooms.

Taco Popcorn

Serves 6 to 8

- *8 cups popped popcorn*
- *3 tablespoons butter, melted*
- *2 teaspoons taco seasoning mix*

Place the popcorn in a large bowl. In a small bowl, mix together the butter and taco seasoning (start with 1 teaspoon and taste before adding more). Drizzle over the popcorn and toss to coat thoroughly. Serve immediately.

*Variation: To make a delicious **Chili Cheese Popcorn**, take 2 tablespoons melted butter, add ½ teaspoon chili powder, ½ teaspoon garlic salt, ¼ teaspoon onion powder, and mix in 8 cups freshly popped popcorn. Serve sprinkled with finely grated Parmesan cheese.*

Popcorn is often shared among friends or family. Many hands in one bowl! Wash those hands with warm soapy water and dry well before partaking, then again after.

Tickled Pink

I love smoothies. They are a quick and easy way to add a variety of fruit to your kids' diets. Here is one of my boys' FAVES!

Makes 2

- *4 cups cold watermelon cubes*
- *2 cups frozen strawberries*
- *½ cup lemon yogurt*
- *1 cup crushed ice*

Pop all ingredients into a blender and blend until smooth.

Variation: Bananas and raspberries make a nice team in a smoothie, as does 1 frozen banana, 5 frozen strawberries, the juice of 1 orange, and 1 cup soy milk . . . Deeeeelish!

 Cut away any damaged or bruised areas on fresh fruit that look rotten and discard.

What's 4 Lunch?

Baby BLTS

Makes 12

- *12 hero rolls (or whole wheat hoagies)*
- *12 slices bacon*
- *¼ head iceberg lettuce, torn*
- *2 tomatoes, thinly sliced*

Preheat the oven to 350°F. Split the rolls without cutting all the way through and bake until just toasted, about 5 minutes. Meanwhile, in a large skillet, cook the bacon until crisp. Drain on paper towels. Just before serving, fill the rolls with bacon, lettuce, and tomato.

Optional: Brush mayonnaise or barbecue sauce inside the rolls before filling.

 Create a BLAT by adding a fresh slice of creamy avocado.

 There are three safe ways to defrost bacon: overnight in the refrigerator, in cold water, and in the microwave. Never defrost bacon on the kitchen counter or at room temperature.

Chicken & Spinach Rolls

This recipe was sent to me from members of the Junior Squad of Golf Queensland. Rising superstars on the course and in the kitchen!

Makes 12

- *14 ounces ground chicken*
- *3 ounces baby spinach*
- *1 can (8.25 ounces) cream-style corn*
- *2 sheets frozen puff pastry, thawed*

Preheat the oven to 400°F. Line a baking sheet with parchment paper. In a large nonstick skillet, place 2 tablespoons water and cook the ground chicken over medium-high heat until cooked through, stirring to break up, about 4 minutes. Let cool, then stir in the spinach and corn, and season to taste. Lay the pastry on a flat, clean surface and cut in half, forming 4 square sheets. Spoon one-quarter of the chicken mixture down the long edge of one piece of pastry. Roll to enclose the filling and cut into three pieces. Gently score the surface of each 3 or 4 times. Repeat with the remaining pieces of pastry and chicken mixture. Place the rolls on the baking sheet seam side down and bake until browned, about 30 minutes.

Optional: Brush with a beaten egg before baking for a glistening shine.

Grated zucchini, carrots, and onions are also fantastic in these.

Chicken Orchard Sammy

Transform the humble sandwich into a lunch box favorite!

Makes 2

- ½ cup shredded poached or roasted chicken
- 4 dried apricots, finely diced
- 2 tablespoons mayonnaise
- 2 slices multigrain bread

In a bowl, mix together the chicken, apricots, and mayonnaise. Use as a sandwich filling for the two slices of bread. Slice the sandwich before serving or wrap tightly and pop it into a lunch box.

Optional: Add a lettuce leaf for color and crunch!

 Bacteria grows rapidly within the temperature range of 40°F to 140°F, so it's always smart to add ice packs to a lunch box, placing them near the food meant to be kept cold.

Cinderella's Pumpkin Soup

Anastasia and Drizella will covet this soup too!

Serves 4

- *1 tablespoon butter*
- *1 leek (white part only), washed and sliced*
- *9 ounces pumpkin or butternut squash, peeled and cut into cubes*
- *2 cups vegetable broth*

In a saucepan, melt the butter. Add the leek and sauté until soft and lightly golden. Add the pumpkin and cook for 2 minutes. Add the broth and bring to a boil. Reduce to a simmer, cover, and cook until the pumpkin is tender, about 30 minutes. Allow the soup to cool slightly before pouring it into the blender. Blend until nice and smooth.

 This soup is equally delicious with additions of corn, garlic, chopped onion and/or potato, and spices such as ground coriander, cumin, and nutmeg.

Fancy Fingers

Stack your Fancy Fingers on top of one another for some amazing Skyscraper Sandwiches!

Serves 2

- *2 slices of your little one's favorite cheese*
- *2 slices ham*
- *6 slices bread, crusts removed*
- *½ cup shredded lettuce*

Place a slice of cheese and ham onto each of two slices of bread. Cover each with another slice of bread, add the lettuce, and top with a final slice of bread. Cut each in thirds and stack one on top of another to serve.

 Use fillings with different textures—softened cream cheese with salmon and dill stirred in; hard-boiled eggs mashed with a little mayonnaise; cottage cheese with raisins, scallions, or pineapple; peanut butter and jelly. All make delicious fillings for these "fingers."

Herby Omelet

Serves 2

- *3 eggs*
- *½ cup grated Cheddar cheese*
- *1 teaspoon chopped fresh parsley or basil*
- *1 tablespoon butter*

In a bowl, beat the eggs. Whisk 3 tablespoons cold water, the cheese, and parsley into the eggs. In a nonstick skillet, melt the butter over medium heat. When foaming, pour in the egg mixture. Reduce the heat to low and cook until the mixture looks set and is golden underneath, 3 to 4 minutes. Use a spatula to carefully fold one side of the omelet over the filling. Cut the omelet into pieces or serve whole. Season to taste.

Tip: The real secret to a perfectly cooked omelet is to cook it over LOW heat. If the heat is too high, the bottom will burn while the middle is still runny. For best results use an 8- or 9-inch high-quality nonstick omelet pan.

Serve with a simple salad of baby spinach, fresh mint, and toasted almonds.

Hot-Diggity Dogs

Makes 4

- *4 hot dogs*
- *1 can (13.7 ounces) baked beans*
- *4 split-top hot dog buns*
- *½ cup shredded white Cheddar cheese*

In a saucepan of simmering water, cook the hot dogs until heated through, 5 to 7 minutes. Meanwhile, in a small saucepan, warm the baked beans. Place the drained hot dogs in the buns and top with the baked beans and cheese.

Try other toppings for the Hot-Diggity Dogs! Make a quick salsa with tomatoes, red bell peppers, and cilantro. Caramelized onions, crispy bacon, and cheese are delicious add-ons, or simply serve with ketchup and mustard.

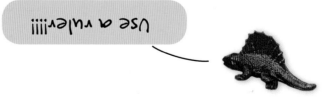

jokE—How do you get straight A's?

Use a ruler!!!

Lunch Box Sushi

Serves 2

- *4 slices multigrain bread (preferably with flax), crusts removed*
- *1 tablespoon mayonnaise*
- *½ avocado, mashed*
- *½ cucumber, thinly sliced lengthwise*

With a rolling pin, gently roll the bread to flatten slightly. Down the middle of each slice, spread a little mayonnaise and avocado. Place cucumber strips on top and roll tightly. Cut into thirds. Pack them tightly into a lunch container cut sides up and with seams touching so the rolls don't spring open.

A variety of fillings can be used for Lunch Box Sushi. Here are some of my favorite combinations:

Avocado, shredded chicken, and thin slices of Swiss or provolone cheese • Cream cheese, salmon, and thin cucumber slices • Cottage cheese, thinly sliced carrots, and raisins • Egg and lettuce • Egg salad • Grated apple, raisins, and cream cheese • Ham, Swiss or provolone cheese, and finely shredded lettuce • Peanut butter and thinly sliced carrot • Tuna, mayonnaise, and finely shredded lettuce

Pizzadilla

I just love this recipe, a clever cross between a pizza (and its yummy flavors) and the cooking style of a quesadilla.

Serves 4

- *2 ounces fresh spinach leaves*
- *⅔ cup shredded mozzarella cheese*
- *4 whole wheat tortillas*
- *1 cup tomato-based pasta sauce, warmed*

Divide the spinach and mozzarella between 2 of the tortillas. Top with the remaining tortillas. Place a nonstick skillet over medium heat. Gently slide 1 pizzadilla into the pan and cook until golden on the bottom, about 2 minutes. Using a spatula, gently flip and cook the other side until the cheese melts, 1 to 2 minutes. Transfer the pizzadilla to a cutting board. Repeat with the second pizzadilla. Cut both pizzadillas into wedges. Serve with the warmed pasta sauce for dipping.

Throw in any number of extra veggies, since it's the melted cheese and tomato dipping sauce that the kids love most. I recommend mashed kidney beans, avocado, finely chopped red bell peppers, corn, and onions.

Quiche Cakes
(for a Lady Bug's Picnic)

Thank you, Ava Roberts (age seven), for naming these little quiches!

Makes 12 ❄

- *2 refrigerated piecrusts*
- *¼ cup ketchup*
- *½ cup grated Cheddar cheese*
- *4 eggs, beaten*

Preheat the oven to 350°F. Using a 2-inch scalloped-edge cookie cutter, cut 12 rounds from the piecrust dough. Gently press a dough round into each of 12 cups of a nonstick muffin tin. Brush each with ketchup Add half the cheese to the beaten eggs, season to taste with sea salt and pepper, and mix well. Divide the mixture evenly among the 12 cups. Sprinkle with the remaining cheese. Bake until golden and set, about 12 minutes.

 Quiches are a superb vehicle for smuggling veggies! Try precooked spinach and broccoli; roasted butternut squash cubes and red pepper flakes; or sliced mushrooms, tomatoes, and onions sprinkled with Parmesan cheese instead of Cheddar. These are all yum-scrum combinations!

Sandwich Rollups

Makes 12 ❄

- *4 slices whole wheat bread, crusts removed*
- *1 tablespoon butter, at room temperature*
- *Sandwich fillings (sliced ham, cheese, pastrami, etc.), your child's favorite*
- *1 bunch chives*

With a rolling pin, roll the bread out until quite thin. Butter lightly and top each slice with your chosen filling(s). Roll tightly, cut into thirds, and tie with a chive.

 A good lunch box sandwich should provide your children with enough energy to sustain them all afternoon. Use sandwich fillings rich in protein: chicken, cheese, ham, and tuna. Loaded with vitamins and minerals: green leafy lettuce leaves, grated carrot, and finely sliced cucumber. Use different types of bread and wraps and cut into triangles, squares, fingers, or roll as shown.

CHILL ❄ *Deli meats are a sandwich staple. To keep them safe, refrigerate until ready to use.*

Spaghetti Cupcakes

This recipe was one of those discoveries that just makes your heart sing. It's versatile, it's delicious, and everyone in the family dives in for seconds.

Makes 12 ❄

- *Olive oil spray*
- *4 eggs*
- *2 cups grated mozzarella cheese*
- *1 can (14.5 ounces) SpaghettiOs*

Preheat the oven to 350°F. Lightly coat 12 cups of a muffin tin with olive oil spray. In a bowl, beat the eggs. Add 1½ cups of the mozzarella and the spaghetti and stir to combine. Using a ¼-cup measure, divide the mixture evenly among the muffin cups. Sprinkle each with the remaining cheese. Bake until the eggs are set and the cheese is lightly browned, about 15 minutes.

Decorate these "cupcakes" with sliced olives, mushrooms, ham, or red bell peppers, or add grated zucchini, carrot, onions, and corn before baking. These will keep in your freezer for up to 2 weeks. Wrap securely in plastic wrap. Simply remove from the freezer to thaw in the fridge overnight, ready for a lunch box with an ice pack the next day.

Click and Cook these yummy Spaghetti Cupcakes with Kim.

Zucchini Slice

Serves 4 ❄

- *6 eggs*
- *1 cup grated zucchini*
- *½ cup self-rising flour*
- *1 cup grated Cheddar cheese*

Preheat the oven to 350°F. Line a 7 x 11-inch baking pan with parchment paper. In a large bowl, whisk the eggs. Whisk in the zucchini, flour, and Cheddar and season to taste with sea salt and pepper. Pour the contents into the prepared pan and bake until set and nicely browned on top, about 25 minutes. Allow to cool slightly, then slice.

 Serve warm with a simple little salad, or refrigerate and save it for the lunch box. Customize it by adding some grated onion, carrot, corn, or sautéed leek or bacon.

jOkE- What's the world's strongest vegetable?

Muscle Sprouts!

5-Minute Fettuccine Carbonara

I love pasta. It's quick, easy, and versatile. And in true Italian style, it's often just a few ingredients that make the best sauces.

Serves 4

- *12 ounces fresh fettuccine*
- *12 slices bacon, chopped*
- *3 eggs, beaten*
- *¾ cup grated Parmesan cheese*

Cook the pasta according to package directions. Meanwhile, in a skillet, cook the bacon until crisp. Drain on paper towels. In a bowl, mix together the eggs and cheese. Drain the pasta, do not rinse, and add it to the egg mixture. Using tongs or a long fork, lift the fettuccine so it mixes easily with the egg mixture, which thickens but doesn't scramble. Add the bacon and toss again. Serve immediately.

 For a nutritious green vegetable, add ½ cup of peas to the fettuccine in the last 1 to 2 minutes of cooking.

Beef & Plum Stir-fry

Stir-frying is a cooking technique where food is cooked quickly in hot oil, but I have often found that it cooks just as nicely in a marinade or sauce.

Serves 4 ❄

- *½ cup plum sauce*
- *1 tablespoon mustard*
- *1 pound beef for stir-fry*
- *1 cup raisins*

In a frying pan, combine the plum sauce, mustard, and ¼ cup water and bring to a boil. Add the beef and cook over high heat for 8 minutes. Add the raisins and cook for another 2 minutes.

Add thin strips of red or green bell pepper or scallions to the stir-fry and serve over white or brown rice. What could be simpler?

Click and Cook this hearty stir-fry with Kim and Morgan.

Beef Stroganoff

Daddy makes this all the time; it's quick, easy, and tasty.

Serves 4

- *1 pound beef for stir-fry*
- *1 packet (1.5 ounces) beef stroganoff sauce mix*
- *8 ounces cream cheese, at room temperature*
- *8 ounces cremini mushrooms, sliced*

Heat a nonstick skillet over medium-high heat and lightly brown the beef. Add the sauce mix and ½ cup water and simmer gently for 30 minutes. Add the cream cheese and stir until it melts and makes a creamy, gravylike sauce. Add the mushrooms and simmer until they are soft and tender, about 5 minutes longer.

Serve over brown rice to soak up the deliciously rich and inviting sauce, along with your kids' favorite veggies like asparagus and carrot. Garnish with some sliced scallions.

Cha-Cha Enchiladas

Enchilada literally means "enchilied," in this case dipped in chili sauce. Choose a mild enchilada sauce if you are making this for your kids for the first time.

Makes 10 ❄

- *10 (8-inch) flour tortillas*
- *2 cups shredded roast chicken*
- *1½ cups shredded Monterey Jack or Cheddar cheese*
- *1 can (10 ounces) enchilada sauce*

Preheat the oven to 350°F. Warm the tortillas in the microwave for 30 seconds or until soft. Divide the chicken among the tortillas, roll up, and place in a baking dish. Top the tortillas with ¾ cup cheese. Pour the enchilada sauce on top and sprinkle with the remaining cheese. Bake until the topping is golden and bubbling, about 30 minutes.

 This is the perfect veggie smuggler dish—the kids can't see what you smuggle into the enchiladas! Smashed kidney or pinto beans, chopped tomatoes, onions, garlic, or diced olives all blend beautifully. Serve with a sprinkle of fresh cilantro . . . *yum, yum!*

Easy Peasy Fish Cakes

I am forever looking for ways to encourage my kids to eat more fish, and these help immensely!

Makes 8

- *1 cup cooked, flaked fish, e.g., catfish, cod, perch, or tilapia*
- *1 cup mashed potato*
- *½ cup fresh or frozen peas*
- *1 egg*

In a bowl, mix together the fish, potato, peas, egg, and sea salt and pepper to taste. Roll into 8 balls. Chill for 30 minutes before heating a nonstick skillet over medium heat and lightly frying. Cook for 3 minutes on one side, then flip and cook for 3 minutes on the other side.

 Go crazy with the herbs and veggies in these savory cakes. Grated carrot, finely chopped scallions, a little lemon zest, chopped parsley, and corn are some of my favorites.

Always keep meat, poultry, fish, and eggs refrigerated at or below 40°F and frozen food at or below 0°F.

Mac 'n' Cheese

This is a timeless classic. Kids big and small around the world like mac 'n' cheese, especially when the accompanying salad makes up the hair, eyes, and mouth ☺.

Serves 4 to 6 ❄

- *1 cup shredded Cheddar cheese*
- *4 cups cooked elbow macaroni*
- *2 cups heavy cream*
- *2 eggs, beaten*

Preheat the oven to 325°F. Measure out ¼ cup of the Cheddar cheese and set aside. In a bowl, combine the remaining cheese, the macaroni, cream, and eggs; season with sea salt and pepper. Mix well and pour into a 6-cup (or similar-size) baking dish and bake until the sauce thickens, 35 to 40 minutes.

 Adding some peas, corn, cooked mushrooms, ham, and finely diced carrot never hurt anyone!

Click and Cook this gooey mac 'n' cheese with Kim.

Meat Loaf Cupcakes

Every time I see this photo, it makes me smile. Isn't food just wonderful? It allows us to be so creative, easily turning a staple meat loaf into gorgeous cupcakes!

Makes 12

- *1 pound ground beef*
- *1 egg*
- *2 slices multigrain bread, grated*
- *¼ cup barbecue sauce, plus extra for basting*

Preheat the oven to 350°F. Line 12 cups of a muffin tin with foil liners. In a large bowl, combine the beef, egg, bread crumbs, and ¼ cup barbecue sauce. Divide the mixture evenly among the muffin cups. Brush the tops with a little barbecue sauce and bake until cooked through, 20 to 25 minutes. Remove from the oven and let rest.

Optional: For the "icing," spoon some warmed mashed potato into a large ziplock bag. Cut off the tip of one of the bottom corners and pipe the potato onto the top of each meat loaf in a swirling motion to ice your "cupcakes."

 The options are endless, but some of my favorite smuggling ideas are finely chopped celery, onion, grated carrot, and beets seasoned with fresh thyme.

Popeye's Pie

When I first served this to my kids, I encouraged them to try it by telling them about Popeye, Olive Oyl, and poor old Bluto. They looked at me quizzically and asked, "Who are they?" Haha! How old did I feel?

Serves 8 ❄

- *1 sheet frozen puff pastry, thawed*
- *3 eggs*
- *1 cup ricotta cheese*
- *2 to 3 ounces baby spinach (about 2½ cups packed)*

Preheat the oven to 350°F. Line a 9-inch quiche dish with parchment paper or lightly spray with olive oil. Fit the pastry into the dish. In a bowl, whisk the eggs, then mix in the ricotta. Add the spinach and season with sea salt and pepper. Pour the mixture into the pastry and bake until the eggs are set, about 30 minutes.

 Pies and quiches are a great way to hide veggies. Onion, garlic, oregano, corn, and pine nuts all taste terrific in this scrummy pie.

 When cooking egg mixtures, cook until the center of the mixture reaches 160°F. Cool, then freeze. Simply defrost in your fridge overnight. Most cooked foods, or leftovers, stored in the refrigerator should be used within 3 to 4 days.

Porcupine Balls

Can you believe this was one of the first recipes I learned to cook in my high school home economics class of 1983? And I'm still making it!

Serves 6

- *1¾ pounds ground beef*
- *2 eggs, beaten*
- *⅔ cup long-grain white rice*
- *3 cans (10.75 ounces) condensed tomato soup*

Preheat the oven to 375°F. In a bowl, combine the beef, eggs, and rice, and season with sea salt and pepper. Mix well and form into 1½-inch meatballs. Place in a large baking dish and cover with the soup. Take each can and swirl with 3 to 4 tablespoons water. Add this liquid to the meatballs. Cover and bake until the ground beef is cooked through and the rice is tender, about 50 minutes. Remove the lid for the last 15 minutes.

 Serve with mashed potatoes and steamed veggies like broccoli and carrots. For extra veggie content, add some grated zucchini or finely chopped fresh herbs to the ground beef mixture.

 The safe minimum internal temperature for ground beef is 160°F; use a food thermometer to be sure. Otherwise, it could be exposed to harmful bacteria.

Quick 'n' Easy Pasta Bake

One night I asked my then eight-year-old what he thought of this dish.
He said he'd write it down . . . it's the accompanying note in this photo ☺.
Too cute, huh?

Serves 4 ❄

- *12 ounces fresh cheese tortellini*
- *2 to 2½ cups pasta sauce*
- *½ cup freshly torn basil leaves*
- *1 cup shredded mozzarella cheese*

Preheat the oven to 350°F. Cook the tortellini according to package directions. Drain and toss with the pasta sauce, basil, and half the cheese. Season to taste with sea salt and pepper. Pour the mixture into a baking dish and sprinkle with the remaining mozzarella. Bake until the cheese is golden brown and bubbling, 15 to 20 minutes.

Add some nutrients to your pasta sauce—pureed pumpkin, sweet potato, parsnip, and carrots are all delightfully delicious.

Cutting boards need to be maintained and monitored for cleanliness. They should be washed with hot soapy water or placed in the dishwasher.

Sammy Salmon Pasta

This super simple recipe was shared by a friend whose little boy, Sammy, absolutely *looooves* it.

Serves 2

- *4 ounces angel hair pasta*
- *4 broccoli florets or crowns, quartered*
- *½ cup heavy cream*
- *7 ounces salmon fillet, baked or grilled, broken up into small pieces*

In a medium pot of boiling water, cook the pasta according to package directions. Meanwhile, in another pan, bring 1 cup water to a boil. Add the broccoli and cook until tender, about 4 minutes; drain well. Return to the stovetop over medium heat and add the cream and salmon, stirring gently for 2 minutes, or until warm. Drain the pasta, add to the creamy salmon mixture, and toss to combine.

Variation: Here is another really simple, kid-friendly salmon recipe: Marinate salmon steaks in teriyaki sauce in the fridge for at least 2 hours. Place the salmon in a lightly oiled baking dish, drizzle with the teriyaki marinade, and sprinkle with a teaspoon of brown sugar (1 teaspoon sugar for each salmon steak). Bake in a 350°F oven until the salmon flakes easily, about 30 minutes. Spoon the pan juices over the salmon before serving . . . Yummy!

Sticky Lamb Chops

These are a great way to ease your kids into spicier foods. Adjust the amount of Thai sweet chili sauce according to their little taste buds.

Serves 4

- *2 tablespoons soy sauce*
- *3 tablespoons Thai sweet chili sauce*
- *8 lamb chops*

In a bowl, mix together the soy and sweet chili sauces. Preheat the broiler or a grill to high and cook the chops for 2 minutes on each side, or to a safe internal temperature of 145°F as measured with a food thermometer. Reduce the heat to medium-low (or move to indirect heat on the grill) and continue cooking for 2 to 3 minutes while brushing with the tasty baste. Cover loosely with foil and let rest for 3 minutes before serving.

Serve with creamy mashed potatoes and greens, or roasted peppers, sweet potatoes, and zucchini.

Although this is not used as a marinade, it could easily be. If you are marinating beef or lamb for the grill, remove the meat from the marinade, and use the liquid to make a yummy sauce by bringing it to a boil just before using.

Click and Cook these tender lamb chops with Kim and Dylan.

Sweet Chicken Fingers

These are just sensational! My family requests these for dinner at least every other week. Quick, easy, and healthy ☺.

Serves 6

- *2 cups cornflakes, crushed*
- *1 cup shredded Parmesan cheese*
- *¾ cup plain yogurt*
- *2¼ pounds chicken tenders*

Preheat the oven to 350°F. Line a baking sheet with parchment paper. In a shallow bowl, combine the cornflakes and Parmesan. Place the yogurt in a separate shallow bowl. Coat the chicken with the yogurt and then roll in the cornflake mixture. Place on the baking sheet and bake until the chicken is cooked through and the coating is golden and crunchy, about 15 minutes.

 Serve this with potato salad and corn on the cob, or mashed potatoes, peas, and roasted cherry tomatoes.

 Click and Cook these tasty chicken fingers with Kim.

Tempura Fish Bites

Kids generally love "bite-size" anything.

Makes 16

- *1 pound fish fillet, e.g., catfish, cod, perch, or any other firm fish*
- *1 cup cornstarch*
- *1 egg*
- *½ cup vegetable oil*

Cut the fish into ¾ -inch cubes (you should have about 16). Pop the cornstarch into a medium bowl. Stir in the egg and ¾ cup of really cold water until just combined. Let the batter sit for a few minutes. In a large skillet or wok, heat the oil until shimmering but not smoking. Dip the fish cubes in the batter, allowing the excess to drip off. Working in batches (so as not to overcrowd the pan), fry for 6 to 7 minutes, or until golden brown, turning once. Drain on paper towels.

*Optional: Add 1 tablespoon lemon juice to the batter to create yummy **Lemony Fish Bites**, and substitute really cold seltzer or club soda for the water if you have any.*

Tomato Drummies

I absolutely love easy and economical, and both are present in this scrumptious dish.

Serves 4 ❄

- *2¼ pounds chicken drumsticks*
- *1 can (10.75 ounces) condensed tomato soup*
- *1 packet (1.5 ounces) French onion soup mix*

Preheat the oven to 350°F. Place the drumsticks in a 9-inch square baking dish. Stir together the tomato soup, onion soup mix, and 1 cup water and pour over the chicken legs. Season with pepper and bake for 1 hour until the chicken reaches a safe internal temperature of 165°F as measured with a food thermometer.

Serve with mashed potatoes and steamed green beans and zucchini.

The possibility of bacterial growth actually increases as food cools after cooking because the drop in temperature allows bacteria to thrive. But you can keep your food above the safe temperature of 140°F by using a heat source such as a chafing dish, warming tray, or slow cooker.

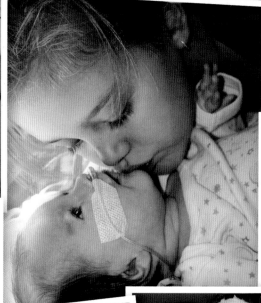

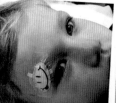

Homemade Takeout

(Why order in when you can make it at home?)

3-Cheese Pizza

One of my personal favorite pizza recipes—melted cheese combined with creamy avocado. *Totally scrummy!*

Makes 2

- *4 ounces mozzarella cheese, shredded*
- *4 ounces feta cheese, crumbled*
- *½ cup grated Parmesan cheese*
- *2 ready-made pizza crusts*

Preheat the oven to 400°F. Divide the three cheeses between the pizza crusts. Bake until the cheeses melt and the crusts are crisp, 10 to 12 minutes. Let cool slightly, then cut into wedges to serve.

 *Top with a tasty **Guacamole:** Take 1 avocado, mash it, and stir in 1 tablespoon chopped red onion, 1 tablespoon chopped cilantro, and 1 teaspoon lime juice.*

 Don't leave pizza out at room temperature for more than 2 hours.

Beautiful Burgers

When this book was released in Australia, my ten-year-old and his "best mate" (as we say in Oz) made these on national TV. Both the boys and the burgers were *fantastic*!

Serves 4

- *1 pound lean ground beef*
- *6 ounces Canadian bacon, finely diced*
- *1 cup shredded Cheddar cheese*
- *½ cup barbecue sauce*

In a large bowl, combine the beef, bacon, cheese, and barbecue sauce. Season with sea salt and pepper and mix well. Form into 4 patties 4 inches in diameter and ½ inch thick. Place the patties on a baking sheet. Cover with plastic wrap and put in the fridge for at least 30 minutes; chilling the patties will help them hold together when cooking. In a large nonstick skillet, over medium-high heat, cook each patty for 4 minutes on each side, or until cooked through.

 Add 1 tablespoon chopped fresh parsley to the mix. Parsley is very high in vitamin C, so add it to meals whenever you can. Serve with a slice of yummy pineapple, tomato, and fresh, crisp lettuce. For a really nice **Turkey Burger***, mix 1 pound ground turkey, 1 small chopped onion, 1 grated green apple, and 1 egg. Mix, chill, and grill!*

Beef & Veggie Pies

These are a great grab 'n' go meal when in a hurry and traveling with kids.

Makes 12 ❄

- *1 pound lean ground beef*
- *2 cups frozen mixed vegetables, thawed*
- *2 cups pasta sauce*
- *4 sheets frozen puff pastry, thawed*

Preheat the oven to 400°F. In a nonstick skillet, brown the beef. Add the veggies and season with sea salt and pepper. Pour in the pasta sauce and simmer for 10 minutes. Meanwhile, cut twenty-four 2½-inch rounds from the puff pastry. Line 12 cups of a nonstick muffin tin with 12 of the pastry rounds. Divide the beef mixture among the muffin cups and top with the remaining rounds of pastry. Seal with a fork. Dust lightly with cracked pepper. Bake until the pastry is nice and golden, about 20 minutes.

 Pies are a terrific way to hide veggies. For the fussiest of eaters you can even puree roasted winter squash, sweet potato, or parsnips and add them to the pasta sauce. They'll never ever know! ☺

 When cooking with ground beef, the center should reach a safe minimum temperature of 160°F. When reheating leftovers, the internal temperature should reach a minimum of 165°F. Use a food thermometer to be sure.

Chicken Nuggets

Whether chicken, fish, or even broccoli, kids just *loooove* nuggets—so give these a try. They are *yummy*!

Serves 2

- *2 boneless, skinless chicken breast halves, cut into bite-size pieces*
- *1 cup mayonnaise*
- *1 cup fine, dried bread crumbs*
- *1 tablespoon butter, melted (optional)*

Preheat the oven to 350°F. Line a baking sheet with parchment paper. Coat the chicken with the mayonnaise and roll in the bread crumbs. Place on the baking sheet. Drizzle with the butter, if using, and bake until golden, 15 to 20 minutes.

CHILL *To keep food safe, nuggets should be consumed, refrigerated, or frozen within 2 hours of baking.*

Healthy Fish Fingers

Serves 4

- *1 pound fish fillet, e.g., catfish, cod, perch, or any other firm fish*
- *2 slices whole-grain bread, grated*
- *¾ teaspoon all-purpose seasoning*
- *1 egg, beaten*

Preheat the oven to 350°F. Line a baking sheet with parchment paper. Pat the fish dry and cut into ¾-inch-wide strips. Combine the bread crumbs and seasoning on a plate. Coat the fish in the egg, then roll in the bread crumbs. Place on the prepared baking sheet and bake until cooked through and crispy, 10 to 15 minutes, turning once halfway through.

*Serve with **Baked Sweet Potato Fries:** Peel and slice sweet potatoes into ⅓-inch-wide sticks. In a large bowl, toss with just enough oil to coat and season. Spread in a single layer on a baking sheet and bake in a preheated 350°F oven for 10 minutes, turn, and bake for another 10 minutes, or until tender.*

jokE - what do whales eat for dinner?

Fish & Ships!

Pita Pizza

Makes 2

- *3 slices bacon, finely diced*
- *4 tablespoons pizza sauce*
- *2 pita breads*
- *½ cup grated mozzarella cheese*

Preheat the broiler to 350°F. In a skillet, cook the bacon for 2 minutes, or until nice and crispy, then drain on a paper towel. Spread the pizza sauce on the pitas, sprinkle with the bacon, and top with the mozzarella. Broil (directly on the oven rack for a crispier crust) until the cheese browns, 8 to 10 minutes.

 This is one of the best veggie-smuggling meals I know. I've even sliced brussels sprouts on it and then watched my babies gobble it up!

 Enjoy pizza with your family by customizing toppings to their individual tastes. Just remember to use one cutting board for fresh produce and one for raw meat, poultry, or seafood when preparing them.

 With leftovers, refrigerate within 2 hours of cooking, store in an airtight container, and consume within 3 to 4 days.

Veggie Ribbon Pasta

I cannot encourage you enough to try this; you will be surprised at how quickly it gets eaten!

Serves 4

- *2 carrots*
- *2 parsnips*
- *2 zucchini*
- *2 cups pasta sauce*

Wash the veggies. Take a veggie peeler and make ribbons out of each. Bring a medium saucepan of salted water to a boil. Add the veggie ribbons and boil until tender, about 3 minutes. Remove and drain. Pop into a large nonstick skillet and season with sea salt and pepper. Pour in the pasta sauce and simmer until warmed through. Serve immediately.

Optional: Serve sprinkled with Parmesan cheese and garnish with fresh basil.

 Be sure to clean vegetables before peeling or using to remove any harmful bacteria.

Wok-On

Serves 4 ❄️

- *1 pound sausage meat*
- *9 ounces egg noodles*
- *¼ cup tamari soy sauce*
- *2 tablespoons honey*

Preheat the oven to 350°F. Line a baking sheet with parchment paper. Using "little hands," roll the sausage meat into meatballs and place on the baking sheet. Bake until golden brown, 10 to 12 minutes. Meanwhile, cook the noodles according to package directions. In a small bowl, combine the tamari and honey. Drain the noodles and transfer to a large nonstick wok. Add the meatballs and sauce and toss over medium heat.

 Okay, the gloves come off when using a wok; they are what vegetables were made for! Cook a variety of freshly sliced or cubed veggies like red bell pepper, or peas and broccoli florets, for color and nutrition, before adding the meatballs.

 Be sure to wash your hands thoroughly before and after rolling the meatballs to avoid the spread of bacteria.

What's 4 Dessert?

4-Minute Strawberry Soft Serve

I don't have an ice cream machine, so for me this recipe is brilliant: easy, creamy, and absolutely 100 percent full of flavor!

Serves 4 ❄

- *10 ounces frozen strawberries*
- *¼ cup superfine sugar*
- *⅔ cup heavy cream*
- *¼ teaspoon vanilla extract*

Combine the frozen strawberries and sugar in a food processor or blender. Process until the fruit is roughly chopped. Add the cream and vanilla and blend until combined. Serve immediately as a delectable soft serve, or freeze for at least 4 hours for a nice firm ice cream.

Variation: The flavors for this are endless. Try it with frozen raspberries, mango, or blueberries; they're all delicious. For a lighter version, replace the cream with your kid's favorite yogurt.

During a power outage, keep the refrigerator and freezer doors closed as much as possible to maintain the cold temperature. This will keep food safely cold for about 4 hours if unopened. Similarly, a full freezer will hold the temperature for about 48 hours (24 if half full) if the doors remain closed.

90-Second Microwave Fudge

Makes 16

- *9 ounces dark chocolate, broken up into small bits*
- *1 can (14 ounces) condensed milk*
- *1 cup chopped walnuts*

Line an 8-inch square cake pan with wax paper. In a large microwaveable bowl, melt the chocolate in 20-second increments, stirring after each, until smooth and creamy. Gradually add the condensed milk, stirring all the while. Add the nuts and stir to combine. Spread the mixture in the cake pan and refrigerate until set, about 1 hour. Cut into 16 squares.

 Although not vegetables, nuts are an important component of the healthy eating pyramid. The special thing about walnuts is that not only do they look like our wrinkled brains, they are very good for our wrinkled brains! They are high in omega-3 fatty acids.

 Click and Make this decadent fudge with Kim.

Banana Splitz

This is how my boys like to eat banana splits. They aren't fans of maraschino cherries or whipped cream. That's the joy of cooking at home; you can customize nearly any recipe to suit your family.

Makes 4

- *4 bananas, whole or split in half*
- *20 mini marshmallows*
- *4 scoops creamy vanilla ice cream*
- *½ cup strawberry sauce (or your child's favorite topping)*

Peel the bananas and place one on each of four serving plates (or banana split dishes). Dot each with 4 marshmallows, dollop with ice cream, and drizzle with strawberry sauce.

Optional: If serving as dessert at a party, add M&M's for a real burst of color. Alternatively, substitute strawberry sauce with your own **Homemade Chocolate Sauce:** *In a small saucepan, melt 7 tablespoons butter over low heat. Add ½ cup light brown sugar, ½ cup heavy cream, and 2 tablespoons unsweetened cocoa powder and stir until well combined, about 3 minutes. Cool a bit before serving.*

Caramel Cookies

Every now and then, you hit on a recipe that you make over and over because it's just so popular. This is that recipe!

Makes 20

- *8 tablespoons (1 stick) butter, at room temperature*
- *½ cup packed light brown sugar*
- *2 tablespoons golden syrup*
- *1 cup self-rising flour*

Preheat the oven to 350°F. In a bowl, cream the butter and brown sugar. Add the syrup and beat until fluffy. Mix in the flour until the texture is such that you are able to roll into tablespoon-size balls. Place the balls of dough 1 inch apart on a nonstick baking sheet and flatten each gently with the tines of a fork. Bake until golden, 10 to 12 minutes. Cool completely before eating.

Lunch Box Tip: These are lovely in a lunch box and pressed together gently with a little hazelnut spread . . . Deeeelicioso.

Why did the cookie go to the doctor?

It was feeling crummy!!!

Caramel Cupcakes

Cupcakes have never been more popular than they are today, and after you bake this delectable version, you will understand why ☺.

Makes 24 ❄

- *1 cup self-rising flour*
- *1 can (13.4 ounces) dulce de leche*
- *1 egg*
- *⅓ cup butter, at room temperature*

Preheat the oven to 350°F. Line 24 mini muffin cups with paper liners. Sift the flour into a bowl and add the caramel, egg, and butter. With an electric mixer, beat until pale and fluffy, about 2 minutes. Divide the batter among the cups and bake for 10 minutes, or until a skewer inserted into the center comes out clean. Let stand in the pan for 5 minutes before transferring to a wire rack to cool.

Optional: For a dazzling finish, top with a **Simple Ganache:** *Make by warming 1 cup heavy cream and adding 9 ounces dark chocolate to it, stirring until the chocolate melts and combines. Garnish with a slice of your favorite chocolate candy bar.*

Chocolate-Coated Ritz

Coat individual crackers with chocolate *or* dip some halfway. It's the lovely combination of sweet and salty that makes these simply irresistible.

Serves 4

- *4 ounces dark chocolate, broken into pieces*
- *16 Ritz crackers*
- *2 tablespoons peanut butter*

Line a baking sheet with parchment paper. In a microwaveable bowl, microwave the chocolate in 20-second increments, stirring after each, until nice and smooth. Take 2 crackers, spread one with peanut butter, and top with the other. Dip the "sandwich" in the melted chocolate, turning to coat completely. Gently shake to remove any excess chocolate. Repeat with the remaining crackers. Refrigerate until the chocolate is set, about 30 minutes.

Dot 2 Dot Cookies

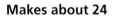

Just try and stop at one ... or two!

Makes about 24

- *1 box (18 ounces) devil's food cake mix*
- *8 tablespoons (1 stick) butter, melted*
- *2 eggs*
- *4 ounces M&M's*

Preheat the oven to 350°F. Line 2 baking sheets with parchment paper. In a large bowl, combine the cake mix, butter, and eggs and mix. Using a tablespoon, dollop spoonfuls of the mixture onto the baking sheets, 1 to 1½ inches apart to allow for spreading. Gently press to flatten with the tines of a fork and top each with four M&M's. Bake until the cookies are set, about 10 minutes. Remove from the oven and allow to cool and harden.

 Click and Bake these colorful cookies with Kim and Flynn.

Heaven in a Cookie

These are *S.E.N.S.A.T.I.O.N.A.L!*

Makes 18

- *1 pint vanilla ice cream, softened*
- *⅔ cup crunchy peanut butter*
- *18 soft-baked chocolate cookies*

In a large bowl, beat the ice cream and peanut butter with an electric mixer until nice and smooth. Pour the mixture back into the vanilla ice cream tub and freeze. Meanwhile, preheat the oven to 350°F. Place each cookie flat side up onto the top of each cup of a cupcake tin. Pop them into the oven for 5 minutes to soften them. Remove from the oven, then carefully press the cookies down into the cupcake cups. Let cool in the pan. When ready to serve, dollop a scoop of the deliciously creamy peanut butter ice cream into each "cookie cup."

*Optional: Serve drizzled with **Hot Fudge Sauce** (see page 132).*

Jell-O Cocktails

When the girls from my office come over with their kids for dinner on a Friday night, this is the dessert they always request. (The kids like it, too!)

Makes 20

- *3 packages (3 ounces) raspberry gelatin dessert*
- *1 envelope (.25 ounce) unflavored gelatin*
- *1 cup heavy cream*

In a heatproof pitcher, stir together the gelatin dessert and plain gelatin. Add 3 cups boiling water and stir until the gelatin is dissolved. Cool for 5 minutes, then stir in the cream. Pour into a wax paper–lined 9 x 13-inch baking pan or 20 cocktail cups and refrigerate until set, at least 4 hours.

*Optional: Make this treat even prettier with a **Rose Petal Chip** garnish: Simply place some rose petals onto a paper-lined baking sheet. Brush lightly with egg white and sprinkle with superfine sugar. Leave overnight to dry.*

M&M's Bars

According to my boys, this is one of the world's yummiest bars. I'm pretty sure it's one of the easiest ☺!

Makes 16

- *2½ cups graham cracker crumbs*
- *1 can (14 ounces) condensed milk*
- *1 cup M&M's*

Preheat the oven to 325°F. Line an 8 x 4-inch loaf pan with parchment paper. Pour the graham cracker crumbs into a large bowl. Add the remaining ingredients and combine well. Scrape the mixture into the prepared pan. Bake for 20 minutes. Let cool in the pan, then cut into 16 *scrum-diddily-umptious* bars.

 Click and Bake these chewy M&M's bars with Kim and Ava.

Milky Way Slice

Isn't it funny how life turns full circle? My brothers and I just loved this scrummy slice when we were little, and now our kids do, too.

Serves 6

- *2 Milky Way bars (4 pieces), chopped*
- *4½ tablespoons butter*
- *3 cups Rice Krispies cereal*

Line a 7 x 11-inch baking pan with wax paper. In a microwaveable bowl, melt the candy bars and butter in 20-second increments, stirring after each, until the mixture is smooth. Add the Rice Krispies and mix well. Press into the prepared pan. Refrigerate for 1 hour, or until set, then cut into slices when ready to serve.

There are no seven wonders of the world
in the eyes of a child.
There are SEVEN MILLION!

—*Walt Streightiff*

Sensational Sundae

Serves 4

- *8 scoops creamy chocolate chip ice cream*
- *1 cup skinned hazelnuts, chopped*
- *1 cup chocolate-hazelnut spread (like Nutella)*
- *2 Flake chocolate bars (use any "flaky" chocolate bar, or Twix or Twirl)*

Layer 4 serving glasses with the ice cream, hazelnuts, and the spread. Top with half a chocolate flake on each, and serve immediately!

*Optional: Try my aunt's famous **Hot Fudge Sundae**. In a saucepan, combine 1 can (14 ounces) condensed milk with 4 ounces dark chocolate and cook over low heat, stirring, until nice and smooth, about 3 minutes. Cool slightly. Place a scoop of vanilla ice cream into four serving glasses and divide half the chocolate fudge sauce among them. Add another scoop of ice cream and the rest of the fudge sauce. Serve immediately, garnished with fresh strawberries or raspberries.*

You can never be too full for dessert.

—*Kelly, age 4*

Toblerone Slice

Honestly, I will be in your life for a very *loooooooooong* time with this dessert. It's just lovely lovely lovely!

Makes 12

- *2 sticks (8 ounces) butter, at room temperature*
- *⅔ cup sugar*
- *2¼ cups all-purpose flour*
- *2 bars (3.52 ounces each) Toblerone milk chocolate, broken into pieces*

Preheat the oven to 325°F. Line a 7 x 11-inch baking pan with parchment paper. In a bowl, with an electric mixer, cream the butter and sugar until soft. Add the flour and gently mix until combined. Pat firmly into the baking pan and bake until the top turns a light golden color, about 20 minutes. Remove from the oven and immediately sprinkle the broken pieces of Toblerone over the top. Leave for 5 minutes, then using a spatula or flat spoon, spread the softened chocolate evenly over the base. Refrigerate to cool and set for at least 1 hour. Using a hot knife, cut into scrumptious slices.

Best-Ever Ice Cream Cake

This is my SUPERSTAR CAKE for any occasion. Kids big and small, adults—in fact *everyone* loves this cake!

Serves 12

- *2 quarts chocolate mint ice cream, slightly softened*
- *14 ounces crunchy chocolate cookies, roughly crushed*
- *2 pints fresh strawberries, halved*

Press half the ice cream into an 8-inch springform pan to form your first layer (about 1 inch thick). Make sure you spread the ice cream right to the outer edges. Top with a layer of crushed cookies. Place a layer of strawberries over the cookies (reserve a handful for garnish), then press in the remainder of the ice cream and sprinkle with the rest of the crushed cookies. Press a piece of foil onto the top of the ice cream cake. Freeze the cake overnight. The following day, release the sides of the springform pan and run a spatula or a long, bladed knife around the edge of the cake. Place a serving plate on the top of the cake and quickly but gently turn the cake over. Remove the base, decorate quickly with the reserved strawberries and broken chocolate cookies, and serve immediately.

Bugs in Rugs

My mum remembers making these for my tenth birthday party (to which I proudly wore a royal blue dress with white polka dots—yes, it's true, I retain a lot of useless information). In Australia, they are called Bugs in Rugs. You might know them as Pigs in Blankets.

Makes 12

- *3 slices whole wheat bread, crusts removed*
- *½ cup ketchup*
- *12 cocktail franks*
- *4 tablespoons (½ stick) butter, melted*

Preheat the oven to 350°F. Spread the bread with the ketchup, then cut the bread into quarters. Pierce the franks all over with a fork. Place a frank diagonally on each piece of bread. Bring up the edges and secure with a toothpick. Brush liberally with the melted butter. Place on a nonstick baking sheet and bake until the bread is crisp and lightly browned, about 10 minutes. Serve warm.

Caramel Popcorn

Scrum-diddily-umptious!

Serves 6

- *8 cups popped popcorn*
- *½ cup honey*
- *½ cup smooth peanut butter*
- *3 tablespoons butter*

Place the popcorn in a large bowl. In a small saucepan, boil the honey for 5 minutes. Stir in the peanut butter and butter. Pour over the popcorn and mix well to coat.

Variation: A savory option is to buy buttered microwave popcorn, pop it, pour into a large bowl, and coat with grated Parmesan cheese and a sprinkle of paprika.

Corn for popping can be stored in an airtight container for about a year. I have read that it is best stored in the refrigerator or freezer because the kernels will retain more of their natural moisture and pop up larger and fluffier.

Chocolate Crackles

A quick, easy, and truly delicious recipe from the beautiful Melanie Roberts, one of the lovely moms who work for me.

Makes 24

- *7 ounces milk or dark chocolate, broken up*
- *8 tablespoons (1 stick) butter, at room temperature*
- *3 cups Cocoa Krispies cereal*

Line 24 mini muffin cups with paper liners. In a large saucepan, combine the chocolate and butter and melt over low heat. Stir in the cereal, coating thoroughly. Divide among the muffin cups and refrigerate for 2 hours to set.

Optional: You could use regular Rice Krispies instead of Cocoa Krispies. Just work with what you have in your cupboard.

Chocolate Fruit Jewels

I cannot tell you how many little girls I've impressed with this easy, elegant recipe. 4 Ingredients will be in your life for a *looooong* time with this little gem!

Serves 8

- *9 ounces milk chocolate, broken up*
- *½ cup colored sprinkles*
- *8 ounces seedless grapes, washed and dried*

Line a baking sheet with wax paper. In a microwaveable bowl, melt the chocolate in 20-second increments, stirring after each, until smooth and creamy. Fill a small cup with sprinkles. Using a toothpick or a fork, dip each grape completely in chocolate and shake gently to remove the excess. Then dip or roll in the sprinkles and place on the baking sheet. When they are all done, pop them in the fridge to set the chocolate, about 20 minutes.

 Click and Make these gorgeous Chocolate Fruit Jewels with Kim and Ava.

Fizzy Cupcakes

My dear friend Melanie Roberts introduced me to this clever recipe. Soda pop, because of the carbonation, adds leavening to these cupcakes; it also adds flavor and moisture. They truly are the *easiest cupcakes* I have ever made.

Makes 12

- *1 box (18.25 ounces) yellow or white cake mix*
- *1 can (12 ounces) soda pop (I used cream soda)*

Preheat the oven to 325°F. Line 12 cups of a muffin tin with paper liners. Pour the cake mix into a large bowl. Add the soda and stir with a wooden spoon until combined. Divide the mixture evenly among the muffin cups. Bake for 12 to 15 minutes, or until a skewer inserted into the center comes out clean. Let stand in the pan for 5 minutes before transferring to a wire rack to cool.

Tip: Remember that in this recipe you are substituting seltzer or soda pop for eggs, oil, butter, and sugar. They are fabulously fast to make! Serve as is or topped with a simple **Cream Cheese Frosting:** *Put 1 stick butter, 8 ounces softened cream cheese, 3 cups confectioners' sugar, and a splash of vanilla extract into a bowl and beat until smooth and creamy . . . Super yummy!*

Grape Wands

Who ever thought something so simple could be so magical? Honestly, when my beautiful sister-in-law made these for my nephew's fifth birthday party, I was speechless. Why had I never thought of this before? They were the hit of the day, consumed even before all of the sugary treats.

Makes 12

- *8 ounces green grapes*
- *8 ounces red grapes*

Thread the grapes onto 12 wooden skewers. For visual effect, vary the colors, some green, some red, some red and green.

Variation: Instead of skewers, you could try plastic toy wands (sanitized, of course) from your local dollar store. A perfect way to lure all the princess partygoers to the fruit!

When you want something expensive, ask your grandparents!

—*Matthew, age 12*

Heart Me Toasties

Makes 6

- *6 slices whole wheat bread*
- *2 tablespoons butter*
- *½ cup shredded Cheddar cheese*

Lay each slice of bread onto a flat, clean surface and butter just one side. Using a heart-shaped cookie cutter, cut two hearts from each slice. Flip six hearts over and sprinkle with cheese on the unbuttered side, then place the other six hearts on top, butter side up, to create little heart-shaped sandwiches. Lightly toast each in a sandwich press or in a nonstick skillet over medium heat until nice and golden. Gently push a skewer into the bottom of each heart. Serve immediately.

Tip: For a really cute party presentation (see the photo), place an orange in a pretty gift box and gently press the skewers in it to hold firm. Then drape with ribbon to hide the orange.

Jelly Fish

These were the toast of my three-year-old's party last year. His little friends adored them.

Makes 8

- *1 box (3 ounces) lemon gelatin dessert*
- *4 ounces gummi fish candy*
- *1 box (3 ounces) Berry Blue gelatin dessert*

Prepare the lemon gelatin as per the package instructions and fill the base of 8 glasses evenly. Refrigerate for 30 minutes, then gently push a fish into the gelatin (I used a skewer to push it beneath the surface). Refrigerate until set. Prepare the Berry Blue gelatin as per the package instructions and divide evenly among the 8 glasses. Refrigerate for 30 minutes, then gently push another fish into the gelatin. The gelatin needs to be nearly set when you put the fish in, otherwise your fishy will float to the top like it ain't feelin' too well—if you know what I mean. Refrigerate for at least 3 to 4 hours to set completely.

*Variation: Amanda Smith, my lovely cousin, shared this easy suggestion, something she calls **Snake Pits:** Make 2 packets of green gelatin as per the package instructions and pour into 6 little plastic wine goblets. Leave to cool for 20 minutes before adding 2 gummi snakes to each cup, ensuring their heads are hanging out over the edges. Refrigerate for a few hours to set. The kids love them!*

Octopus Dip

This is my ten-year-old's all-time *faaaavorite* dip. It took me several months to get around to trying it, but when I did, I sure made up for lost time. It's *fun-tastic*!

Serves 8

- *½ cup mayonnaise*
- *½ cup sour cream*
- *1 clove garlic, crushed through a press*
- *1 red bell pepper*

In a bowl, mix the first three ingredients together and season with sea salt and pepper. Cover with plastic wrap and refrigerate for 15 minutes. Meanwhile, cut the bottom third off the bell pepper to be the body of the octopus, and slice 8 long strips from the bottom two-thirds for tentacles. When ready to serve, spoon the dip into a dish, place the octopus's head in the center, and surround with his 8 legs.

 I love this dip because it pairs perfectly with fresh, raw veggie sticks (carrots and celery), broccoli florets, or cauliflower. Give your octopus googly eyes with blueberries held in place with toothpicks. You could also use raisins.

Partysicles

Packed with your kid's favorite fruits, each bite bursts with flavor. They are a healthy, colorful addition to any birthday party, and best of all, they can be made in advance!

Makes 8

- *4 ounces strawberries, cut into smallish cubes*
- *¼ small cantaloupe, rind removed, cut into smallish cubes*
- *1 kiwifruit, peeled and cut into smallish cubes*
- *2 oranges, juiced*

In a bowl, combine the strawberries, cantaloupe, and kiwifruit and mix thoroughly. Spoon into ice pop molds or plastic cups and divide the orange juice among them. Freeze for 4 to 5 hours or until set.

*Optional: Pop any leftover fruit into little plastic cocktail glasses and serve as **Fruitilicious Cups**.*

Peanut Butter & Chocolate Shards

This is almost too good for words. That glorious combination of chocolate and peanut butter is to die for!

Serves 8

- *14 ounces white chocolate, coarsely chopped or broken*
- *1¾ cups chunky peanut butter*
- *14 ounces milk or dark chocolate, coarsely chopped*

Line a 7 x 11-inch baking pan with parchment paper. In a microwaveable bowl, microwave the white chocolate and peanut butter together in 30-second increments, stirring after each, until nice and creamy. Pour the mixture into the baking pan, spreading evenly. In a second miocrowaveable bowl, repeat with the milk chocolate. Drizzle the melted milk chocolate over the peanut butter mixture. With a knife, draw swirls. Refrigerate until set and then cut into shards to serve.

Princess Pops

I bought the decorative sticks for my Princess Pops online, or you can get your little princess busy designing, drawing, and cutting her own pretty princess faces and taping them to pop sticks. This is also a great little girls' party activity!

Makes 30

- *21-ounce store-bought moist fudge cake with chocolate frosting*
- *14 ounces white chocolate*
- *1 teaspoon vegetable oil*
- *½ cup pink cake decorating beads (nonpareils)*

Into a large bowl, break up the cake and frosting and mix together until combined. Using wet hands, roll the mixture into balls 1 inch in diameter, then press gently on either side, molding each ball into a bell shape. Place on a baking sheet, pushing down gently to flatten the base. Continue until all the mixture is used. Place the bells in the freezer for 1 hour. Just before removing, break up the white chocolate into a large microwaveable bowl and microwave in 30-second increments, stirring after each, until the mixture is nice and smooth. Add the oil and stir well to thin the chocolate (this makes it easier to work with). Place the cake decorating beads in a small dish. Using a fork, dip each bell into the white chocolate. Drain off the excess chocolate, then dip in the pink beads to cover the base and just up the sides to form the border of the princess's gown! Place back on the baking sheet, then gently press a Princess Pop into the top until she's sitting neatly on her princess gown.

Rainbow Rolls

Makes 4

- *4 slices pastrami*
- *1 cup cooked white or brown rice*
- *½ avocado, cut into thin strips*
- *1 carrot, cut into thin matchsticks*

Place the pastrami slices on a clean, flat work surface. Place the rice along the middle of each slice. Lay the avocado strips and carrot sticks on top of the rice. Roll up the pastrami and secure with a toothpick. Serve as is or sliced in half.

 Use any number of the following fillings: corn, cucumber ribbons, thinly sliced red bell peppers, sliced omelet, hummus, green beans, sliced snow peas, toasted almonds, and mashed sweet potato.

Scrolls

Honestly, what can I say about these gloriously easy scrolls? Please, if you've never had them before, try this recipe, as it is bound to become a family fave ☺.

Makes 24 ❄

- *2 square sheets frozen puff pastry, thawed and halved*
- *¼ cup tomato sauce or spaghetti sauce*
- *4 ounces ham, chopped*
- *1 cup shredded Cheddar cheese*

Preheat the oven to 400°F. Line 3 baking sheets with parchment paper. Working with one sheet at a time, place a sheet of puff pastry on a clean cutting board. Spread with the tomato paste and sprinkle with the ham and cheese. Starting from the edge nearest you, roll up the pastry. Cut each roll into quarters, then cut each quarter in three. Place the scrolls, cut side up, onto the baking sheets ¾ inch apart. Bake until the pastry is golden and the cheese melted, 15 to 20 minutes. Allow to cool slightly before serving.

Optional: Brush the pastry scroll tops with beaten egg for a rich, golden finish.

Scrolls are a great way to smuggle all kinds of glorious veggies into the growing bodies of kids. Simply chop and scatter!

Strawberry Garden

For the photograph opposite, I simply placed an orange in the bucket and planted the skewers in it so that they would stand upright. This makes a beautiful centerpiece on any birthday party table.

Makes 24

- *1 pound strawberries, with stems if possible*
- *5 ounces dark or milk chocolate, broken up*
- *½ cup colored sprinkles, chocolate sprinkles, or chopped nuts*

Wash and dry the strawberries (leaving the stems in place). Gently push a wooden skewer into the stem end of each. In a microwaveable bowl, microwave the chocolate in 20-second increments, stirring after each, until nice and creamy. Put the sprinkles in a bowl. Dip each strawberry into the chocolate, rotating it slowly. Lift it out and allow the excess to drain back into the bowl. Stand the skewer in a tall glass or vase. Let cool slightly before dipping into or dusting with the sprinkles. Repeat the process until all the strawberries are coated. Refrigerate for 20 minutes to set the chocolate.

Sweet Sesame Sausages

Watch these fly off the plate at your child's next birthday party—or at any gathering, really. I often pop them into the oven on football afternoons; boys big and small like sausages at halftime!

Serves 4

- *12 breakfast sausage links*
- *2 tablespoons honey*
- *2 tablespoons sesame seeds*

Preheat the oven to 350°F. Line a baking sheet with parchment paper. Arrange the sausage links on the baking sheet and bake for 15 minutes. Drain off any fat. Drizzle with the honey and bake, turning a couple of times, until the sausages are sticky and golden all over, about 10 minutes. Sprinkle with the sesame seeds and bake for a final 5 minutes. Remove, cool, and serve on wooden skewers (to prevent those sticky fingers).

*Variation: For delicious **Mini Meatballs,** take 6 sausages, cut one end of the casing from each sausage, and squeeze a bite-size amount onto a baking sheet. Each sausage should yield around 8 meatballs. Bake in a 350°F oven for 10 minutes, or until cooked. Serve with a little ketchup for dipping and watch them fly too!* ☺

 Click and Cook these delicious sausages with Kim.

PARTY IDEAS

Favors

It's amazing how quickly the cost of filling a favor bag escalates when you are buying several "little" items. Here are a few clever ideas for a lasting memory.

4 Ingredients books

Okay, so I am clearly biased, but buy them on sale and have the birthday child sign each on his or her favorite recipe.

Animals

Buy some inexpensive plastic animals at your local toy, party, or discount store and pop a lovely little thank-you note around their necks.

Books

For each guest, handpick a small paperback or Little Golden Book.

Bubbles

Kids love bubbles!

Crayons and small pads

It may just be what is required to unleash your child's inner Picasso.

Disposable camera

Expect to pay as little as $7 for a 24-exposure disposable camera. Capture the day through the eyes of a child.

Fake tattoos

Come on, Mum, you know you want one, too!

Picture frame

Take a photo of each child with the birthday boy or girl, print it and pop it in the frame to take home.

Piggy bank

Give every child a piggy bank and pop a $1 coin into it.

Plant seeds

A budding gardener may enjoy a pack of tomato seeds or their first mint plant (very hard to kill—it's a good herb to start with!).

Play-Doh

A little tub of Play-Doh is fun for everyone.

Tiaras

Shop around for costume jewelry. There are plenty of bargains out there for future princesses!

Water pistols

Fun for both boys and girls.

Great Party Games

Gods & Goddesses

4+ players

This game requires fairly mellow music. Give each child a book. When the music starts, the children walk around the room balancing the books on their heads. When the music stops, the children must try to go down on one knee. If a books falls, that player is eliminated. The music starts again and the game continues. The last child left in the game is the winner.

I Went to Mars...

6+ players

The children sit in a circle. The birthday child announces, "I went to Mars and I took a . . . " Then names any object (example: "my soccer ball"). The next child has to repeat this and add another example. "I went to Mars and I took a soccer ball and an apple." The third child will add a new object, always keeping the list in order. The game continues around the circle for as long as possible. Whoever slips up the order is eliminated.

Jump the Broom

4+ players

Place a broom on the ground. Play music (note that the person controlling the music should either be blindfolded or be turned around so he or she can't see the kids!) as the children skip around in a circle, jumping over the broom. When the music stops, the child jumping over the broom, or the last child to jump the broom is out. Continue until there is one child left.

Candy Relay

6+ players

Divide the children into two teams and have them form lines. Give the first child in each line a pair of mittens. Give everyone a wrapped hard candy. When you say "Go!" the first player in each line puts on the mittens, unwraps the candy, and pops it into his or her mouth. Then that player quickly takes the mittens off and hands them to the second person in line. The second player does the same, and so on down the line. The team that finishes first wins.

Memory on a Tray

4+ players

Place a number of objects on a tray in no particular order while the children are in another room or focusing on a different activity. A variety of shapes and sizes work best. For example, a paper clip, a quarter, balloon, cookie, envelope, fork, etc. The number of objects included is best dictated by the age of the participants—place more objects for older groups and fewer for younger. When the children are ready, set the tray down for less than 60 seconds (again, this is best dictated by the children's ages) and then remove it from the room. The children then write down each object they remember from the tray. Whoever is able to list the most objects accurately wins! It's always fun to bring the tray back in and remind the group what was there.

Please let us know which of these games you liked playing—and tell us about new ones!—at facebook.com/4ingredientspage.

Acknowledgments

As with all dreams, they are usually realized only with the help and dedication of many. Yes, I had the vision, but the reality came to be with the help of many.

Glen Turnbull, my husband and business partner. If I haven't let you know how wonderful you are, here is a very public declaration: THANK YOU for your ongoing support and belief in me!

Melinda, Michelle, and Kate: Together, may we continue to experience and achieve many amazing things on this journey!

Janelle, Leonie, and Melanie: My R&D team—you EXCELLED on this project (as you do on all of them).

Mom and Dad: You are the best role models for supportive, loving parents any girl could ask for. Love you both xx.

Jan and Michael, my fabulous in-laws. Thanks for always lending a hand whenever asked.

Sarah Branham: THANK YOU for taking a chance on my titles in the United States and for dedicating so much time to this manuscript to make it the best it could possibly be.

To Judith Curr, Ben Lee, Daniella Wexler, Kate Slate, Sybil Pincus, Cristina Suarez, Lisa Sciambra, Diana Franco, Cathy Gruhn, Sandi Mendelson, Sumya Ojakli and her dynamic special sales team at Atria, and everyone else who contributed along the way, it's said lightly, but meant truly: ***"THANK YOU!"***

With love,
Kim

Index

Invitation

Join our Foodie Family

At **4** Ingredients, we have cultivated a family of busy people like you from around the world, all bound together by the desire to create good, healthy, homemade meals quickly, easily, and economically. Our aim is to save us all precious time and money in the kitchen.

We invite you to join our growing family where we share kitchen wisdom daily. If you have a favorite recipe or tip that has worked for you in your kitchen and that you think others would enjoy, please join us at:

 facebook.com/4ingredientspage

@4ingredients

 4 Ingredients Channel

 4ingredients.com.au

@4ingredients

With love,
Kim